Rhythmic Studies for All Instruments Volume 1

by
Tony Moreno

Muse Eek Publishing Company
New York, NY

Copyright © 2006 by Muse Eek Publishing Company. All rights reserved

ISBN 159489-930-4

No part of this publication may be reproduced, stored in a
retrieval system, or transmitted, in any form or by any means,
electronic, mechanical, photocopying, recording, or otherwise,
without the prior written permission of the publisher.

Printed in the United States

This publication can be purchased from your local bookstore or by contacting:
Muse Eek Publishing Company
P.O. Box 509
New York, NY 10276, USA
Phone: 212-473-7030
Fax: 212-473-4601
http://www.muse-eek.com
sales@muse-eek.com

Acknowledgements

Tony would like to thank the following for their help and support: Bruce Arnold, Gabe Cummins, Ronald Andryshak, Marc Mommaas, Rich Mangicaro and everyone at Paiste America for their great support, Bob Moses, Elvin and Keiko, Stan Koor, Nina Dunkel, Emma, Antonio, Gene, and to all of my students and most of all, to Susan and Evan.

About the Author

Tony Moreno is from NYC. He attended and received his degree from the Manhattan School of Music. He studied privately with Stan Koor, Elvin Jones, Bob Moses and Al Kuumba Heath and James Preiss. Tony teaches at New York University, Columbia University and the City College of NY. Tony has appeared on over 70 recordings, and travels extensively throughout the U.S. and Europe.

Foreward

As music evolves, so do the techniques, mechanics and esthetics that musicians use change and develop to express their new approaches to melody, harmony and rhythm. Improvising musicians have been creating and performing music for thousands of years; as musicians who have studied jazz for a number of years can attest, this art form, by its very nature, will continue to evolve. And like all musicians, we draw much of our inspiration through studying the performances of all the great artists throughout the history of our music.

With the continued development of melody, form and harmony, so has rhythm grown to encompass the concepts of many musicians that are introducing challenging new ideas based on meter and form. Since the introduction of African, Afro-Cuban, Indian, South Pacific and Asian music into American culture, musicians have used these influences in both their compositions and improvising.

By applying some of these ideas over standard forms, such as the blues, we can gain an understanding of how these concepts can be applied to many different musical genres. But the idea for many of these exercises is to gain more control over the basic quarter note, of pulse and of form.

These exercises are also meant to be played with other musicians; they are not just solo studies. The best way to learn these concepts is to work in any musical setting you can organize, be it duo, trio or quartet. Often you may want to rehearse in a group setting with a metronome running to help guide the musicians. Once you and your bandmates develop these ideas, begin writing and performing your own compositions and formulating your own ideas.

Table of Contents

Acknowledgements — iii
About the Author — iv
Foreward — v

Counting and Clapping	1
Dotted Quarter Note Transposition of Harmonic Rhythm in "Blues for Alice"	3
Three Bar Cycles of Dotted Quarter Notes	4
Alternate Harmonic Rhythm #1	5
Alternate Harmonic Rhythm #2	6
"Blues for Alice" in Compound Meters	7
"Blues for Alice" in 3/4	8
"Blues for Alice" in 5/4 (3-2 subdivision)	9
"Blues for Alice" in 6/4 (3-3 subdivision)	10
"Blues for Alice" in 7/4 (4-3 subdivision)	11
"Blues for Alice" in 5/4 (short form 3-2 subdivision)	12
"Blues for Alice" in 7/4 (short form 4-3 subdivision)	13
"Blues for Alice" trading 3 bar Phrases	14
"Blues for Alice" trading 5 bar Phrases	15
Subdivisions with accents; subdivisions over a blues form	18
Metric Modulation: triplets and quarter note triplets	24
Metric Modulation on the quarter note triplet level	29
Metric Modulation and Harmonic Rhythm on the quarter note triplet level	30
Harmonic Rhythm in the superimposed 3/4	31
Quarter note triplet phrasing on downbeats and upbeats; introduction to half note triplets	32
Half note triplet harmonic rhythm	34
Half note triplet phrasing with melody	35
Quintuplet subdivisions and Septuplet subdivisions	36
"Blues for Alice" within 5 over 4 Metric Modulation	37
"Blues for Alice" within 7 over 4 Metric Modulation	39

Counting and Clapping

One of the most efficient ways for developing a sense of rhythmic articulation is through the process of counting out loud and clapping. This is best done with a metronome when practicing alone, or in conjunction with another musician. By counting out loud and vocalizing one rhythm while clapping another component of the phrase, we become aware of pulse on an internal level. Rhythm can appear as a three dimensional grid, with different transparencies showing all the interlocking grids of one pattern over another. We can begin to feel rhythm as a dance, albeit a very precise and calibrated structure on which to build variations. Our wish is to create organic phrases that move fluidly, using space and creating drama. When practicing these exercises, always choose tempos that allow you to comfortably hear the patterns. When having difficulty with a particular exercise, it's best to stop and begin reducing the velocity (bpm) until you are able to hear and execute the exercise properly. It is important to keep this in mind when working on new musical ideas: continue slowing down the tempo on the metronome until you can play the beginning measure(s) correctly. Although the mechanics of your performance may seem rigid at these tempos, you must at least "hear" the basic principle before moving forward. And even at these slow tempos, you should continue to strive for musicality, phrasing and articulation.

We will begin by applying a counting system first, and later substitute melody and form as our internal clave. In the same way that drummers would start to work on these exercises within a simple, time-keeping context, rhythm section instrumentalists would begin by comping and counting out loud (with a metronome). We need to hear the original harmonic rhythm and form, as well as altered variations or superimpositions, simultaneously. We begin by understanding these principles as supportive players, dealing with these concepts as accompanists thereby fulfilling and deepening our roles as members of the rhythm section. Once this is accomplished, we have the template for developing our linear (soloing) ideas within this new vocabulary.

It's best to start by using the metronome while counting out loud and clapping the rhythms. When working on a specific rhythmic grouping (such as half note triplets), switch every 4 bars between your original or base meter (the metronome marking every quarter note in 4/4) which you are counting out loud: "1 and 2 and 3 and 4 and" while simultaneously clapping the grouping. It often helps to reinforce the base meter by tapping your foot on each downbeat. You get the 3:4 feeling running through your limbs and voice, similar to how drummers are able to mark time and tempo using a combination of all four limbs. After four bars, you would slightly reverse the process, and count the groupings out loud while clapping and tapping the base meter (4/4). In addition, I've always recommended using your laptop to create your own metronome, click track, sequence, whatever; we have to often think outside the box, so any sequencing software will help you to create your own study loops. But even using the standard metronome, we can assign that instead of representing our base rhythm (quarter notes in 4/4), the metronome is actually counting half note triplets. It then becomes a matter of perception of what we want the metronome to count for us. It can be much more than an eighth or quarter note.

If the base rhythm is 4/4, there are a variety of ways you should practice counting out loud: 1) Counting only the downbeats: 1 2 3 4; 2) Counting the downbeats with eighth note subdivisions: "1 and 2 and 3 and 4 and" 3) Counting the downbeats with eighth note subdivisions and bar numbers: "1 and 2 and 3 and 4 and 2 and 2 and 3 and 4 and 3 and 2 and 3 and 4 and 4 and 2 and 3 and 4 and" . Later, you will have to alter the subdivisions based on your quarter note depending on what type of subdivision or grouping you are working on. If you are working on triplet based subdivisions, you have the following options: 1) Counting only the downbeats: 1 2 3 4; 2) Counting the downbeats with triplet subdivisions: 1-trip-let 2-trip-let 3-trip-let 4-trip-let 3) Counting the downbeats with triplet subdivisions and bar numbers: "1-trip-let 2-trip-let 3-trip-let 4-trip-let 2-trip-let 2-trip-let 3-trip-let 4-trip-let 3-trip-let 2-trip-let 3-trip-let 4-trip-let 4-trip-let 2-trip-let 3-trip-let 4-trip-let". This process would logically continue to 16th note subdivisions, then quintuplets (on the 16th note level), sextuplets (on the 16th note level), septuplets (on the 16th note level), 8 32nd notes, etc.

When counting out loud, we tend to use numbers as our principal means for keeping track of the meter, for hearing the subdivisions, for counting bars when playing a specific form or for trading with the drummer. Of course, there are many systems for counting throughout the world. And they should be explored and incorporated into your practicing regimen. The syllabic systems used throughout the Indian subcontinent, Africa, the Middle East and the South Pacific are highly developed and are easily adaptable to our numerical counting systems. There are a number of books available on this subject, and many are available through the internet. Todd Isler's "Ta Ka Di Mi This" is one of the clearest, thoughtfully written on the South Indian syllabic system. "Ancient Traditions-Future Possibilities" by Matthew Montfort is also beautifully written, and includes chapters on Indian, Balinese and West African rhythms. There are also a number of doctoral studies available through various universities or smaller, independent publishers. Of course, when studying these musical arts there is no substitute for private study with a master musician and teacher who can guide the student properly.
Additionally, there are books written primarily with the drummer in mind, but which are very good for rhythmic sight reading and analysis. Although some are written as etudes for snare drum, and others with the drum set as the medium, you will find a great deal of musical information that is very useful and inspiring. Bob Moses: "Drum Wisdom"; Bruce Arnold: "Odd Meters", The Big Metronome" and "Doin' Time with the Blues"; George Marsh: "Inner Drumming"; anything by Pete Magadini ; Miles Okazaki: "Rhythm Matrix"; all the Gary Chaffee books (three volumes); Gary Rosensweig: "Advanced Rhythms" book #6; Anthony Cirone: "Portraits in Rhythm" and all books by Gavin Harrison.
In our first exercise, we have the melody of Charlie Parker's "Blues for Alice" written on the top ledger line. Below are eighth notes grouped in threes. You will notice that we have a three bar loop of these eighth note groupings; the downbeats of both our original meter and our new grouping lock together every three bars. This is also displayed on the bottom ledger line as dotted quarter notes (you can also think of them as the downbeat of every 3/8 grouping). Over these dotted quarter notes are the chords from the tune but if played as written would create a new harmonic rhythm stretched over the bar lines. The chords are still in their original place, but the value of our new quarter note creates the illusion that the tempo is slowing up very slightly. In addition, our three eighth note groupings begin to sound like triplets in this new feel. You might want to begin by working only with the metronome: set the metronome to 80 bpm in 4/4 and count all the eighth notes: "1 and 2 and 3 and 4 and" while clapping the dotted quarter notes over our 3 bar loop. Then clap quarter notes only (with the metronome at the same setting) while counting the eighth notes "123,123,123, 123". Next, set the metronome to 50 bpm, but now the click is our dotted quarter. Now count our original quarter notes in 4/4 (with eighth notes) over the dotted quarter of the metronome. You may want to count a three bar cycle before beginning to lock up both downbeats. After the properties of these two rhythmic lines have been internalized, we want to add the melody to our new subdivision. With the metronome set at 80 bpm, loop and sing the first three measures of the melody while clapping dotted quarter notes. You may need to straighten out the eighth notes (less of a swing feel) to do this. Later, you will be able to add more of a swing feel by accenting and slightly delaying the second eighth note (the upbeat). But since our three eighth note groupings sound like triplets, you can also add a "rest" on the middle eighth note triplet to strengthen the swing feel with the dotted quarter notes. Once you have the first three measures cycling easily with your singing and clapping, move on to the next three measures of the melody and loop those. Then you'll paste the first six measures together and loop them. Continue this process through the whole form. Once this process becomes clear through singing, counting and clapping, substitute your instrument in place of your voice and repeat the steps above.
I've mentioned how laptops can help us work on rhythmic concepts. In this exercise, you can record the melody with a click. Loop it and alternate choruses between comping in 4/4 and comping with the dotted quarter note subdivision. Next, you could record yourself comping the dotted quarter notes and alternate choruses as above. In both cases, you'll have a chorus where you're locked up, and a chorus where you are juxtaposing one rhythm over another. Again, it should be stressed that we're looking at this idea from the perspective of accompaniment, not as linear solo phrasing, but through comping as part of the rhythm section. We will look at linear applications later on in the book.
A very important rhythmic tool is designating a downbeat every fixed number of bars. In your sequence software , send a click every 2 bars, every 4 bars, every 8 bars, every 12 bars, every 16 bars, every 32 bars.....Please refer to Bruce Arnold's "Doing Time" series and "Big Metronome."

Dotted Quarter Note Transposition of Harmonic Rhythm in Blues For Alice

3 Bar Cycles of Dotted Quarter Notes Grouped as 2 New Measures

This example shows our three bar cycle of dotted quarter notes grouped in 4 as two "new" measures of 4/4 over three of our original pulse. Therefore, we would have eight measures of our new 4/4 over twelve bars of the original form. I have also indicated with accents over beat 1 of measures #1, #4, #7 and #10 the clave or anchor points (thanks Bob!) for our three bar dotted quarter note cycle. It is a good idea of being aware of where different cycles line up depending on the form you're working with. In this case, over a blues form, our locking up points occur in the same places, chorus after chorus. In the case of a 32 bar A-A-B-A form, our cycle would need 24 measures (2 x 12 measures) to lock in to our original beat 1 in the first measure. In other words, both rhythmic lines would converge on the downbeat of measure #25 (the last A section). For the student practicing the exercise at this level, it is recommended to develop both comping and linear phrasing within the dotted quarter note cycle, and round out the last 8 measures of the form by returning to the original 4/4 quarter note. Of course, the next step would be to continue the dotted quarter note phrasing grouped in 4 (our new 4/4) through multiple choruses, without returning to our original quarter until the beginning of the 4th chorus. The relationship of the number three also is apparent on a variety of levels: We are subdividing measures of 4/4 into 3/8 giving us a three bar loop. If we subdivided measures of 4/4 into 6/8 (remember that three is a multiple of six, so we're just looking at a longer grouping), or if we thought of these six eighth notes (a dotted half-note) as our new quarter note, we would have 4 new beats over three measures of our original 4/4. The downbeats would fall on beats 1 and 4 of bar one; beat 3 of bar two; and beat 2 of bar three. We also know that it takes three complete choruses of our dotted quarter note grouped in 4 to return to "the big 1". The relationship of our small subdivision to other, larger patterns remains the same. The number three becomes a constant depending on our point of view. You will see this relationship of a constant through many layers of time as revolving, interconnected gears, all moving at their own rate and each with its own distinctive feel.

Alternate Harmonic Rhythm #1

This example presents the harmonic rhythm slightly anticipated; we are abridging the original harmonic rhythm to fit our template of dotted quarter notes.

Alternate Harmonic Rhythm #2

Another variant with some chords anticipated and others delayed. Since musicians will interpret these ideas in their own unique way, it's always beneficial to review this new harmonic rhythm in slightly altered forms; you could say we'll filter our exercise in a more musical, idiosyncratic way by anticipating how other musicians might hear and phrase these patterns.

Blues For Alice in Compound Meters

The following exercise will present a system of running through various meters over a blues form. This exercise can also be applied over any standard, the only exceptions being compositions that already have mixed meters. Picking a melody and adapting it to fit all the meters will be the first step. Start by picking tunes that you're familiar with and that have simple melodies ("Autumn Leaves", "Stella by Starlight"). As you become more familiar with the process, choose more complex melodic and/or harmonic compositions such as "Confirmation" and "Moment's Notice". When working with complex melodies, you may want to write out the melody for all the different meters, but ideally this should be treated as a visual exercise. Since the melodies have to be altered to fit in each meter, there is no right or wrong way as to how you interpret each measure. Often by adding the appropriate number of rests (or by changing the values of certain notes to make the phrase shorter or longer, or even by drastically editing the melody), you can alter the melody to fit the meter you're in. Practice with a metronome set to constant quarter notes, again choosing a comfortable tempo. It's also a good idea to record yourself when practicing, giving you the opportunity of reviewing your accuracy and phrasing. Play the melody in 3/4, and solo over the form. After soloing, return to the theme and play it now in 4/4, then solo over the form. Repeat this process until you reach the ending meter (7/4) and then cycle backwards to 3/4. You must always play the melody first when moving from one meter to the next before soloing. Although adapting the melody to each meter may prove a little difficult, or some meters will be easier to hear than others, it's very important to begin each new meter not with a solo, but with a statement of the melody. Playing the melody helps to establish and internalize the new meter as well as the accompanying harmonic rhythm. This has to be clear in order to solo comfortably. Your last chorus of soloing in 7/4 would lead you back to the melody played in 6/4. Your last chorus of soloing in 6/4 would lead you back to the melody played in 5/4, and so on. The whole exercise ends up becoming a big loop. This cyclical approach allows for many repetitions of hearing the melody and meter and form move from one meter to the next without stopping. You can always play this exercise in any group setting, trading choruses with the other musicians. It's a good warm up exercise when playing in a session setting.

In our examples we go up through 7/4, although you can apply this to any fixed meter: 9/4, 11/8, etc. Or, you can combine meters in an arranged structure. The first 8 bars of Stella could be arranged as measures of mixed meters: (eighth note = eighth note) measure 1: 7/8; measure 2: 6/8; measure 3: 5/8; measure 4: 4/4; measure 5: 3/8; measure 6: 11/8; measure 7: 7/4; measure 8: 3/4. You could keep this form for the A sections, and create a recurring, alternative set of meters for the bridge.

In the first example, notice that when converting meters from 4/4 to 3/4 the harmonic rhythm remains balanced between both meters. A chord sustained for a full measure in 4/4 (a whole note) becomes a dotted half note in 3/4. If there are two chords sustained for two beats each (a half note) in a measure of 4/4, their new values would be two dotted quarter notes in 3/4.

In the second example, we move to 5/4 as a 3-2 subdivision. This means that each measure of 4/4 in our original piece becomes a measure, with the addition of one extra beat, of 5/4. Notice that the measures are subdivided into 3 beats and 2 beats. This helps us set the harmonic rhythm (as well as the melody) against a predetermined grid. Consequently, a chord sustained as a whole note in 4/4 becomes a dotted half note tied to a half note. Two chords in a measure of 4/4 become a dotted half note (chord one) and a half note (chord two).

Of course, you can invert the quarter note subdivision as a 2-3. This presents the melody and harmonic rhythm in a new light. An interesting exercise is the mirroring of subdivisions within a meter: the first measure of 5/4 could be a 3-2 subdivision and the second measure a 2-3 subdivision; or the first two measures could be a 2-3 subdivision and the following two measures a 3-2 subdivision. Also, remember that we are discussing these subdivisions on the quarter note level. We can also move to smaller subdivisions (micro): eighth notes, triplets, sixteenths, quintuplets, etc. Or larger subdivisions (macro): dotted quarter notes, half notes, etc. All of these can also be treated as 3 or 2 note subdivisions. The possibilities are limitless when improvising.

Blues For Alice in 3/4

Blues For Alice in 5/4 (3-2 subdivision)

Blues For Alice in 6/4 (3-3 subdivision)

This example presents the piece in 6/4. Because this is evenly divided in a 3-3 subdivision, our 1 measure chords are a dotted whole note (or two, tied dotted half notes) in 6/4. Likewise, two chords in our measure of 4/4 become two dotted half notes.

Blues For Alice in 7/4 (4-3 subdivision)

This example presents the piece in 7/4 as a 4-3 subdivision on the quarter note level. Our 1 measure chords in 4/4 (whole note) are now 7 beats in length. Two chords in 4/4 (two half notes) now become a whole note (4) and a dotted half note (3) in one measure of 7/4.

Blues For Alice in 5/4 (short form 3-2 subdivision)

The following example presents a condensed form of 5/4. In this system, you take the first original measure of your composition (4/4) and convert it to 3/4 (dotted quarter note = 3 beats). The second original measure (4/4) is converted to 2/4 (half note = 2 beats). Combine both measures to give you one large measure of 5/4. Notice the following: that we are using the 3-2 subdivision; and that because of our rhythmic compression, the harmonic rhythm moves at a faster rate; if there is one chord in your measure of 3/4, then you play a dotted half note; if there are two chords in your measure of 3/4, divide the bar evenly into two dotted quarter notes; if your measure of 2/4 has one chord, it is played for the duration of a half note; if your measure of 2/4 has two chords, divide the bar evenly: each chord will be a quarter note in duration. In addition, the same study of subdivisions would apply here as in our previous example in 5/4: reversing the subdivision to 2-3; alternating 4 measures of the 3-2 subdivision with 4 measures of the 2-3 subdivision; mirroring each grouping: 2-3-3-2 or 3-2-2-3.

Blues For Alice in 7/4 (short form 4-3 subdivision)

The following example presents a condensed form of 7/4 (as a 4-3 subdivision). In this system, you take the first original measure of your composition (4/4) and leave it in its original meter (whole note = 4 beats). The second original measure (4/4) is converted to 3/4 (dotted half note = 3 beats). Combine both measures to give you one large measure of 7/4. Notice the following: that we are again using the 4-3 subdivision; and that because of our rhythmic elasticity, the harmonic rhythm moves at a faster rate only in the second measure; if there is one chord in your measure of 4/4, then you play a whole note; if there are two chords in your measure of 4/4, divide the bar evenly into two half notes; if your measure of 3/4 has one chord, it is played for the duration of a dotted half note; if your measure of 3/4 has two chords, divide the bar evenly: each chord will be a dotted quarter note in duration. In addition, the same study of subdivisions would apply here as in our previous example in 7/4: reversing the subdivision to 3-4; alternating 4 measures of the 4-3 subdivision with 4 measures of the 3-4 subdivision; mirroring each grouping: 3-4-4-3 or 4-3-3-4.

Blues for Alice Trading 3 Bar Phrases

The ability of controlling form is essential to all improvising musicians. Form gives us the parameters in which we work. And yet form can take many different shapes. Within a form there might be sections that are open and continue until cued. Form may not even be rhythmic in nature, but based more on melodic form and/or harmonic color. Exercises for developing this control can take many forms, but these exercises will deal with a blues form. They can be easily adapted for any standard tune. Trade 2 choruses of 4 bar phrases with another musician and then at the top of the form on the third chorus trade 2 choruses of three bar solos (the following example) and loop the entire form.

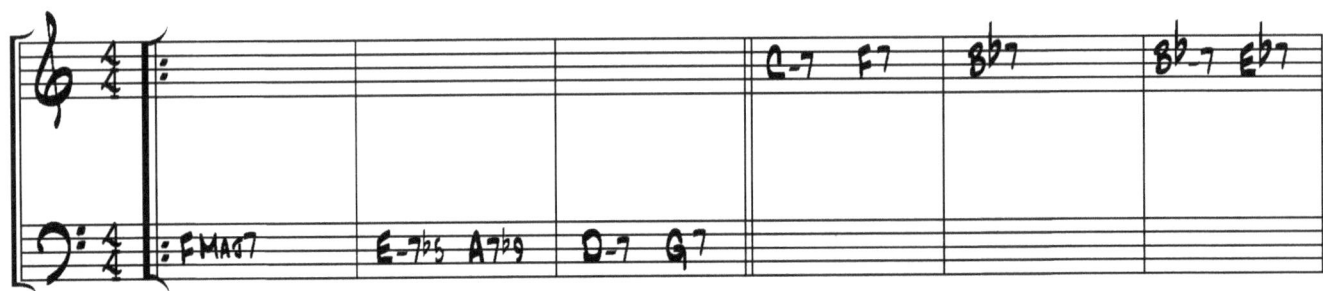

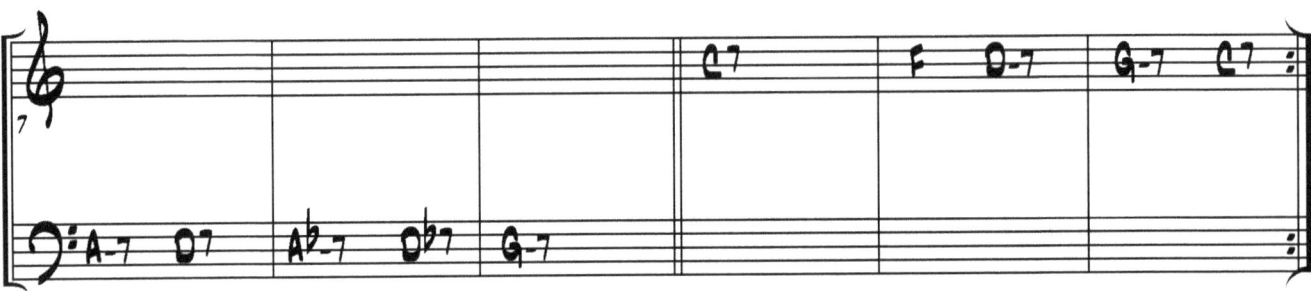

Blues for Alice Trading 5 Bar Phrases

Now we'll trade 5 bar phrases over a blues form. Notice that it takes five complete choruses to cycle back. Although in the beginning the trading of 3 and 5 bar phrases may seem mechanical and forced because of the focus needed in maintaining your place in the form, over time you will see the shape that these phrases have both within the overall form and as separate units. Of course, you can apply larger units for trading: 6, 7, 8 or 9 bars. And this exercise applies to standards as well. Another approach to form exercises is where you reduce the total number of bars from your original composition by a fixed number of bars (or beats). For example, "Stella" could be played as a 7 bar tune; just cut out the last measure of every eight bar phrase (28 bar form instead of 32). You would do this both for the melody and soloing. Or "Donna Lee" as 5 measures per section instead of 8; both the melody and soloing. Or a blues where the form is 11 bars in length? Or the last measure of your blues is in 3/8? How fluid and organic is your phrasing within these new rhythmic forms and harmonic rhythms?

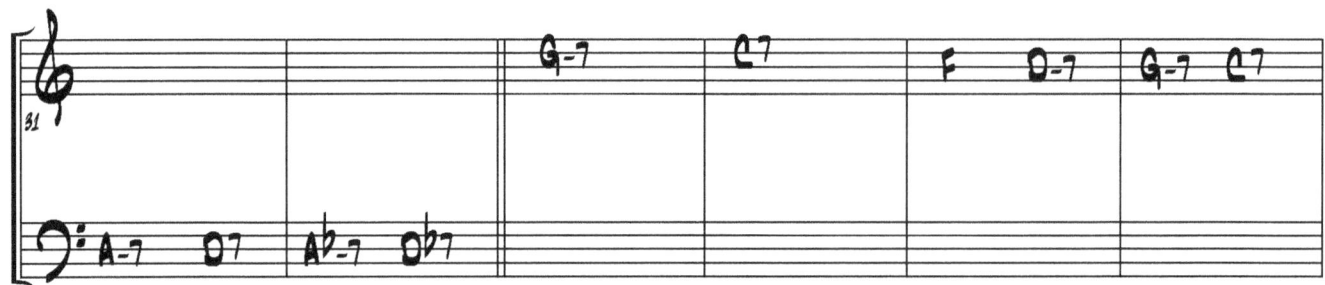

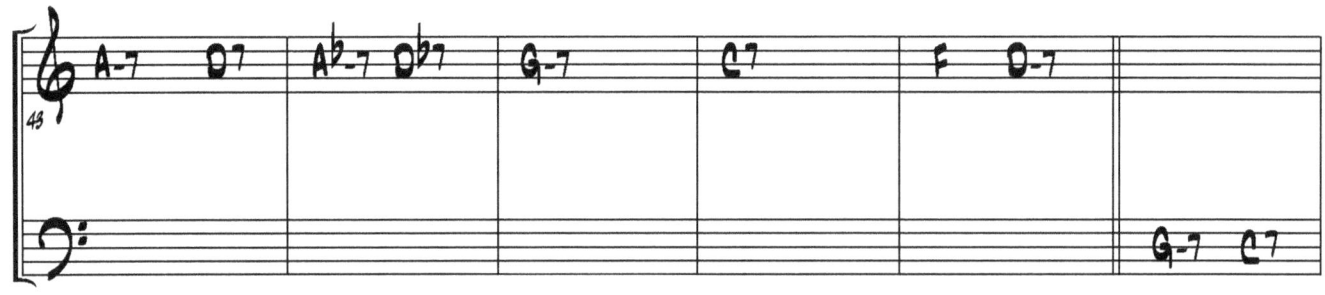

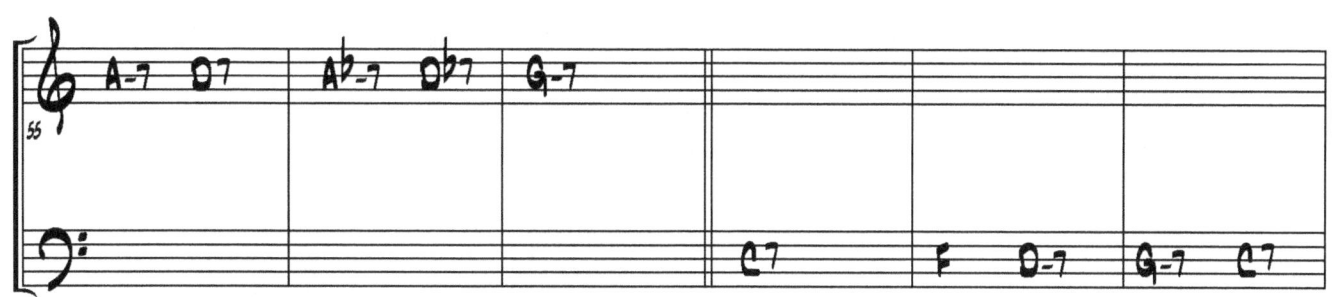
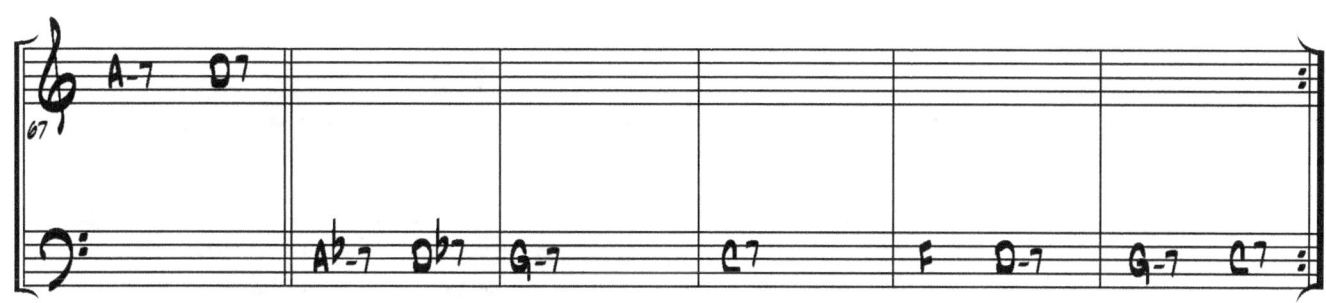

In this exercise, set the metronome at a comfortable tempo. Since we want to here all the subdivisions of the quarter note clearly, you will want to make sure that your 32nd note phrases can be executed clearly. Articulation is very important, especially when we begin adding accents.

This is a soloing exercise based over a blues form. Every 4 bars will introduce a new subdivision. For the 16th note quintuplet and septuplet, you may want to write out your solo, or at least your subdivision. Of these groupings:

Running through all 4 choruses of the blues form will return to the eighth note level. One musician comps while the other solos; after completing an entire form, players switch roles. Begin at very slow metronome levels = 30-40 bpm.

This study will help in hearing all the subdivisions over one quarter note.
Repeat each line 12 times (12 bar blues).

Play linear phrases for the entire cycle: all eighth note lines with the corresponding accent. When returning to the top of the form, comp only an accented note hearing the rest of the measure filled out with rest(s).
Then move on to the next level (triplets) and follow the same process. The same system can be applied to sextuplets, septuplets, etc.

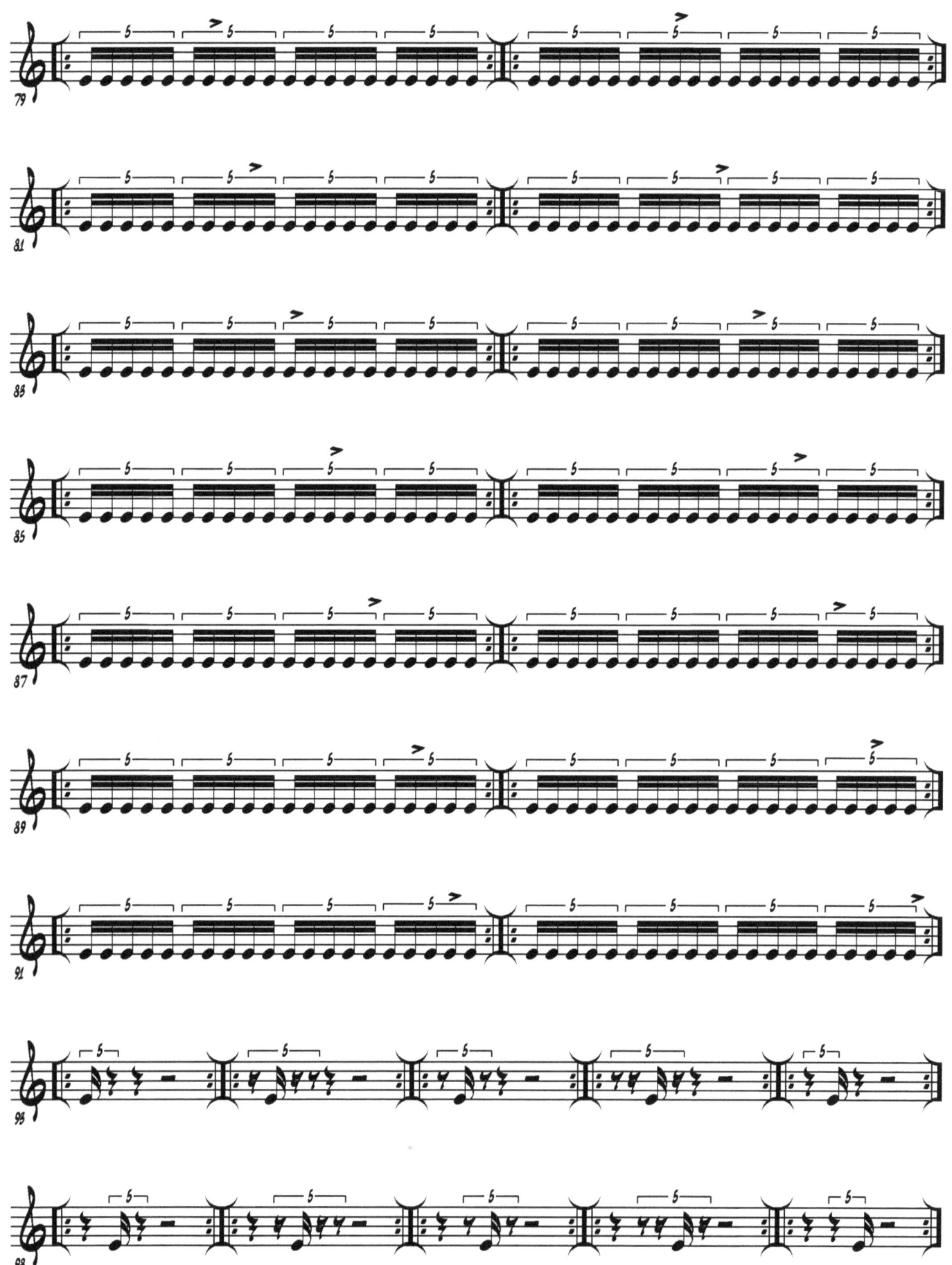

22

The accent points that have only the accent notes and rests may be approached in a different way. If we treat the solitary accent as the "point of departure" for our phrase, or to put it another way, "our starting point," begin your phrase on that accent, ending before its return. Conversely, if we treat the accent as our "point of return," you can begin your musical phrase anywhere in the measure, and conclude it on the accent point. In Bob Moses' "Drum Wisdom," the whole idea of accent points and how Bob assigns an extra measure for development between each point is a very important work on the subject and presents these ideas in a more musical light. Another aspect of dealing with subdivision is to reduce them to their most common denominator. If we have a measure of sixteenth notes in 4/4 we can subdivide them as follows:

The subdivision could be considered in different ways:

1

But our lowest common denominator would include just the longest and shortest subdivisions:

1

This principle is also referred to as the long/short beat subdivision. The short beat would be any 2 beat subdivision, and the long beat any 3 beat subdivision

In 7/8 we can subdivide:

In 11/8 we can subdivide:

In both cases, we have subdivided everything into long and short beats,

Karl Berger, at the Creative Music Studio in Woodstock, presented a syllabic system based on the long beat: "GA-MA-LA" and the short beat:"TA-KI". In 9/4, you can count the 3 beat groupings as 3 long beats:

Or as a different subdivision:

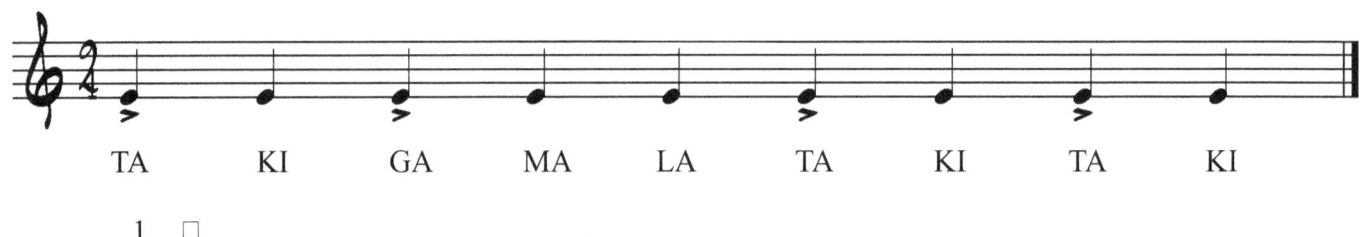

For further study, "Rhythm Matrix" by Miles Okazaki is strongly recommended.

#1) Eighth note triplets subdivided into the corresponding quarter note triplets; it can also be written with the eighth notes tied together. Practice counting the triplets from one level to the next with the metronome marking quarter notes. Try converting the metronome to mark quarter note triplets while you count (and play) in 4/4.

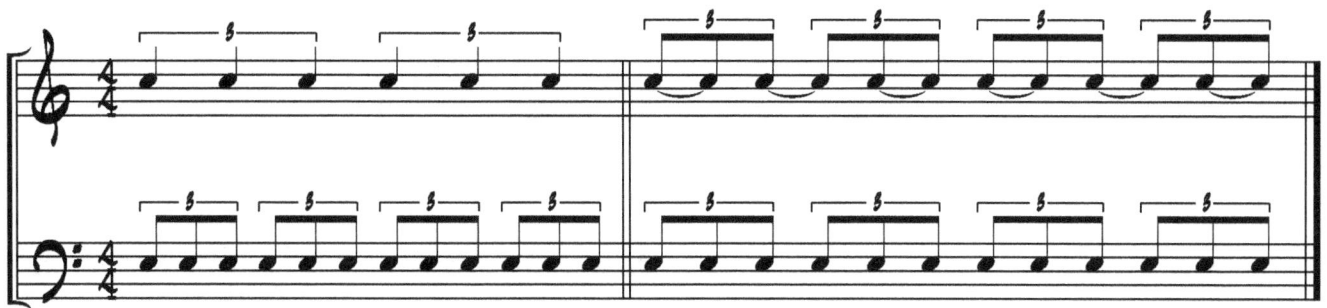

#2) If counting the triplets in groups of six, accent the quarter note triplets by marking the first, third and fifth beats.

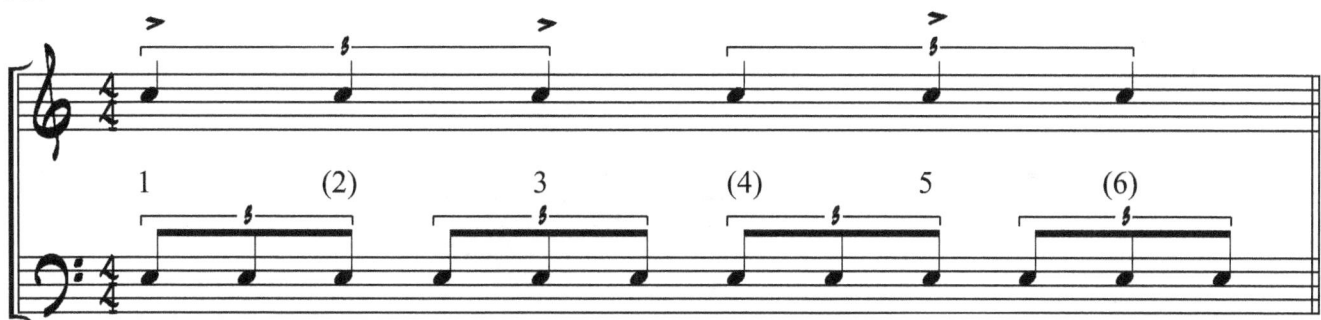

#3) Both systems of notation represent the same rhythmic phrase.

#4) Set the metronome to mark quarter note triplets. Count the down beats out loud for 4 measures, then the downbeats and upbeats. Try running through both a straighter eighth note feel (more duple based) and a swung (triplet based) feel when phrasing the eighth notes. Clap the quarter note triplets.

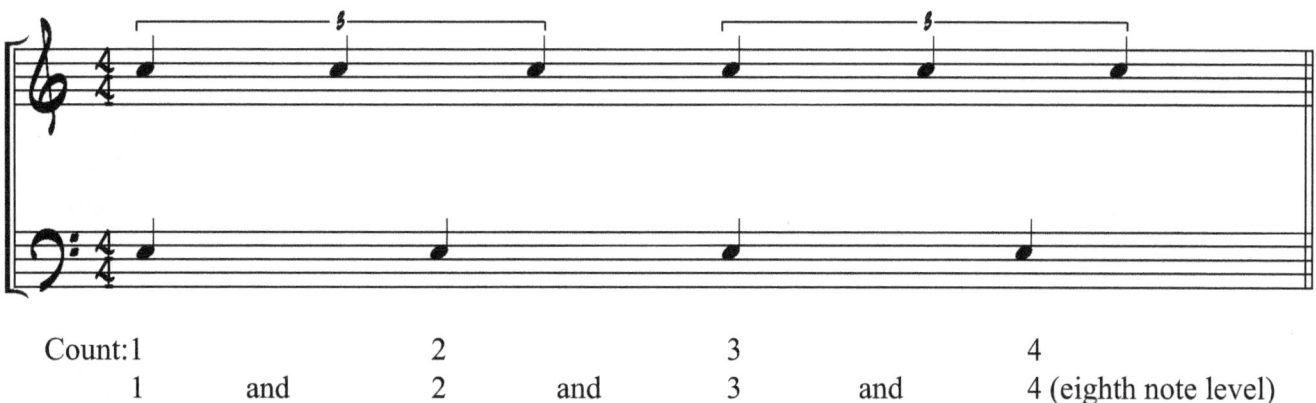

Count: 1   2   3   4
       1   and   2   and   3   and   4 (eighth note level)

#5) With the metronome marking quarter notes, count out loud all the quarter note triplets at each level for 2, 4 or 8 bars. At a later date, we will look at these relationships over compound meters; i.e. quarter note triplets grouped in threes within 3/4; 4/4; 5/4; 6/4; 7/4, etc. Or, quarter note triplets grouped in 4,5,6,7 note groupings over 3/4; 4/4, etc.

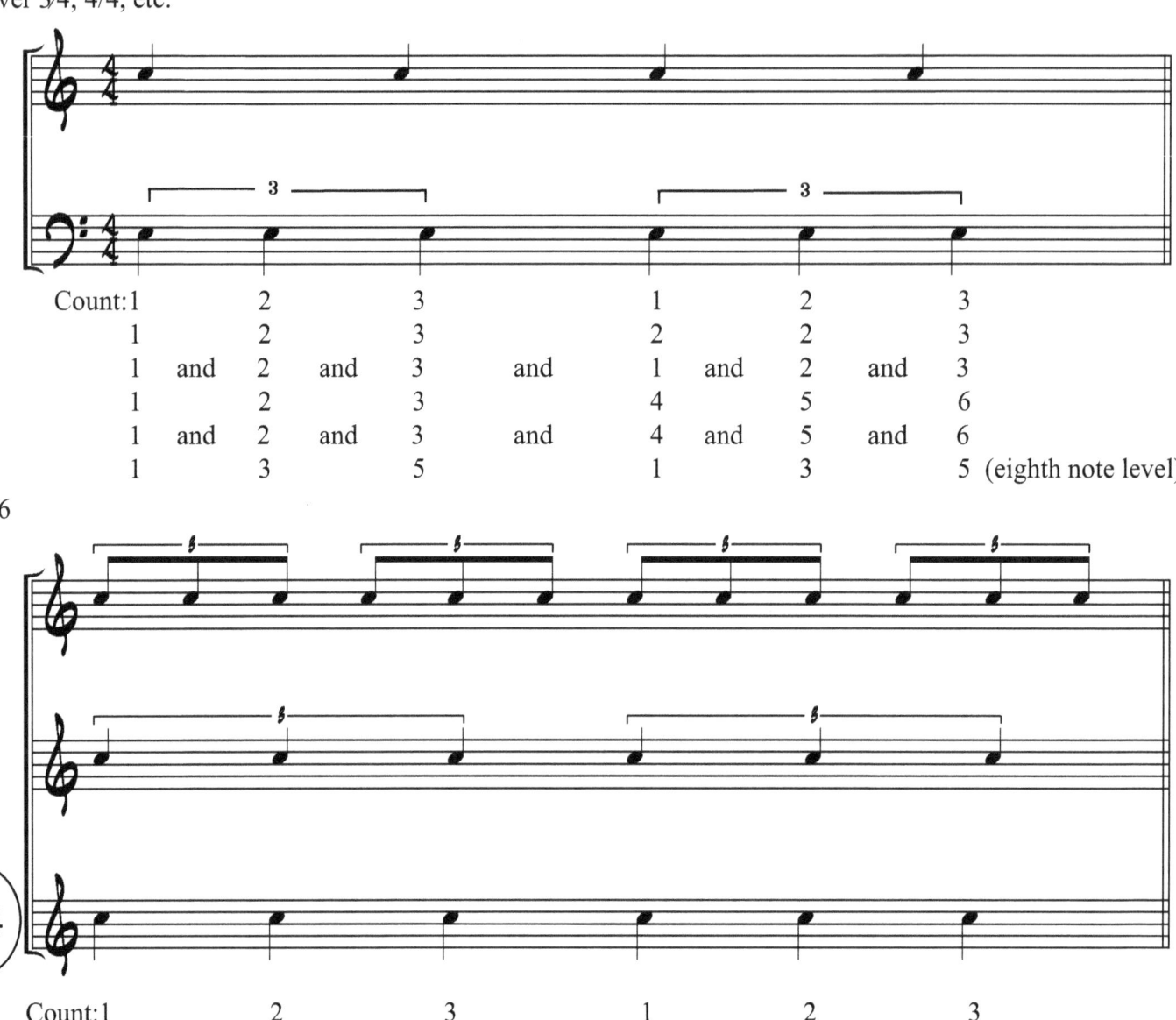

These examples will break the quarter note triplets (as our new quarter note) into eighth notes.

Example 1) Count the upper line with the metronome marking quarter notes. Accent the "1" as you count. The accents alone also represent quarter note triplets beginning on a downbeat.

Example 2) Now repeat the step for example 1 but accenting the "2", or upbeat, of the quarter note triplet. The example below is the upbeat accent alone or quarter note triplets starting on an upbeat.

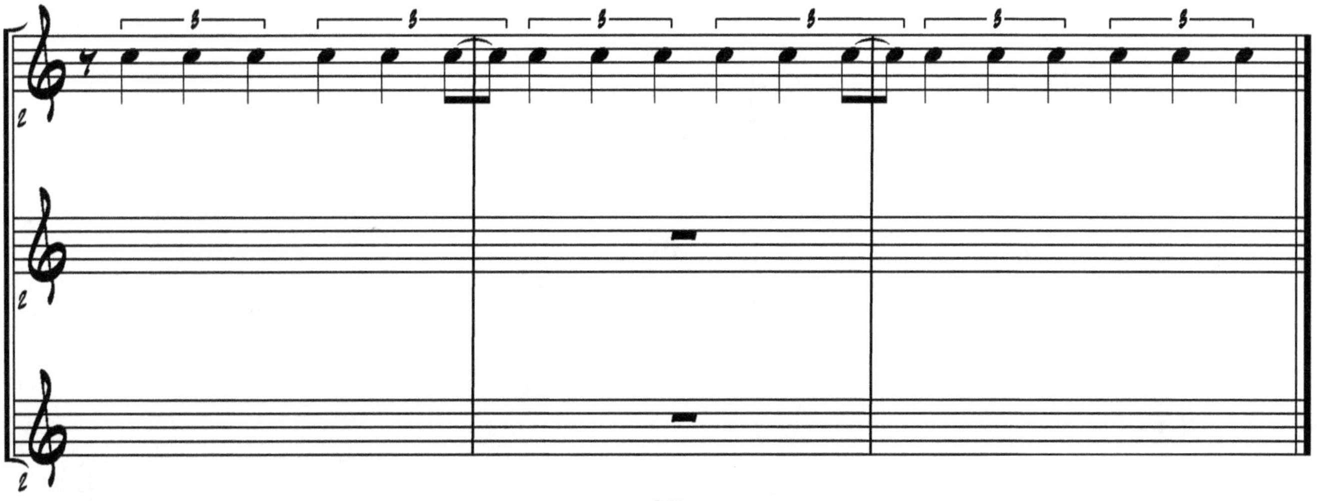

Example 3) Now the quarter note triplets begin on the third eighth note triplet of beat one, and how it would be written with the accent alone.

When subdividing the eighth note triplets into quarter note triplets (where the quarter note = one quarter note triplet), we can superimpose a three (or six) feel over the original form. The upper level shows the eighth note triplet subdivision into quarter note triplets, or 6 over 4. These are then subdivided symmetrically as represented by the broken line. If there is one chord per measure in the original form, then there is one chord for all six quarter note triplets. Two chords in the original form translate into three quarter note triplets each. The harmonic rhythm can also be altered over the quarter note triplet feel in other groupings: 4-2; 2-4; 5-1; 1-5, etc. The lower level shows the harmonic rhythm rewritten as the new three feel. Note that in the new 3 feel our form is now 24 measures long. With a 6 feel, our new form is 12 bars long.

24 Bars of New 3/4 or 12 Bars of new 6/4

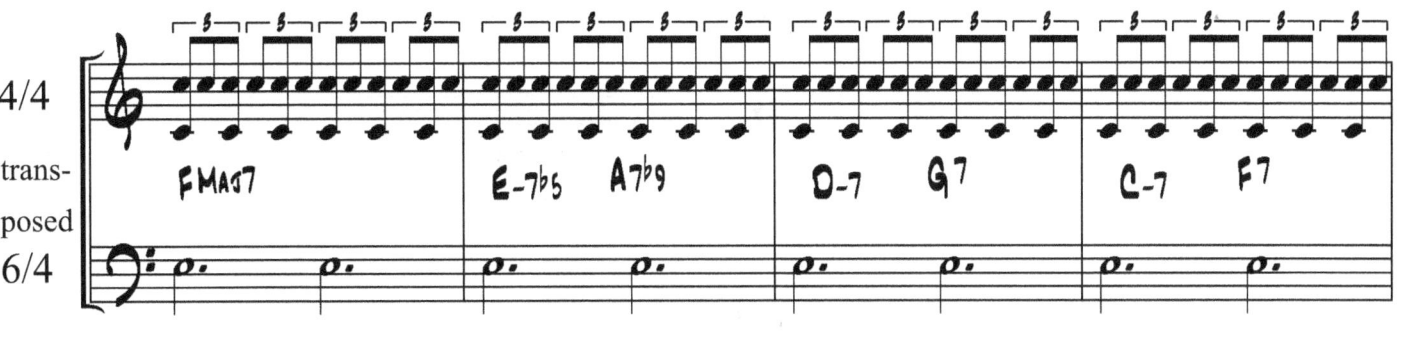

Here is the quarter note triplet subdivision in 4 note groupings. Remember that our original quarter note is equivalent to a quarter note triplet. Note that if we retain the harmonic rhythm in its original form we will have some interesting groupings. The lower level shows the harmonic rhythm rewritten to fit the new template: 1 new measure of 4/4 over FM7; 2 beats of the second new measure continues with the first beat on E-7♭5; and the third measure continues with the first beat on E-7♭5, and the remaining three beats over A7♭9. Of course, all the chords that are 3 new beats in length (A7♭5, F7, E♭7, D♭7 and C7) can be anticipated by one beat to give a more balanced 4/4 feel. Note that in this 4 beat grouping we have 18 measures of new 4/4 over our original 12.

Harmonic Rhythm in the Superimposed 3/4

These examples are to be played with the metronome marking all quarter notes while counting out loud and clapping the accents. Since the 4 note grouping of quarter note triplets in the previous example may prove difficult, before progressing to the half note triplet feel practice counting the triplets as groups of 4; the syllabic equivalent in Indian counting is written out as well. The following examples displace the accent to all four points.

The next example shows the eighth note triplet level as it relates to quarter note triplets and half note triplets. Practice counting 4 bars each from one level to the next.

The following examples illustrate some methods of counting and clapping.

ta ka di mi ta ka di mi ta ka di mi

Example 1) Counting quarter note triplets as our new quarters and eighths; and with the downbeats accented (our new quarter note).

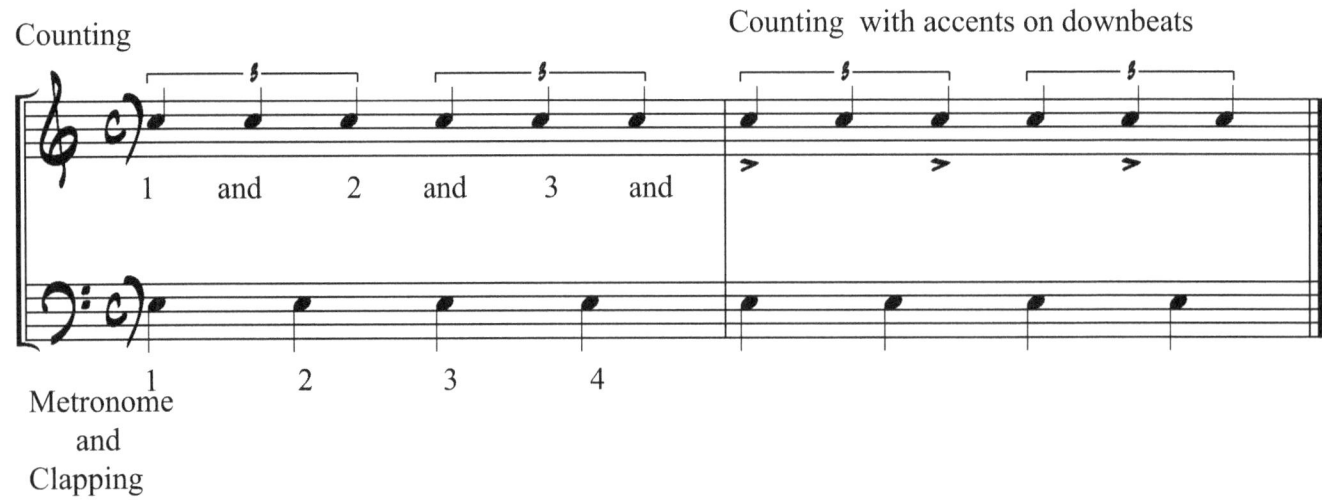

Example 2) Counting quarter note triplets as quarters and eighths with accents on the upbeats; and counting only the half note triplets with the metronome marking quarters. This is example is very important if we consider the upbeats swung, or slightly delayed, within the context of jazz phrasing in 4/4 with eighth note upbeats.

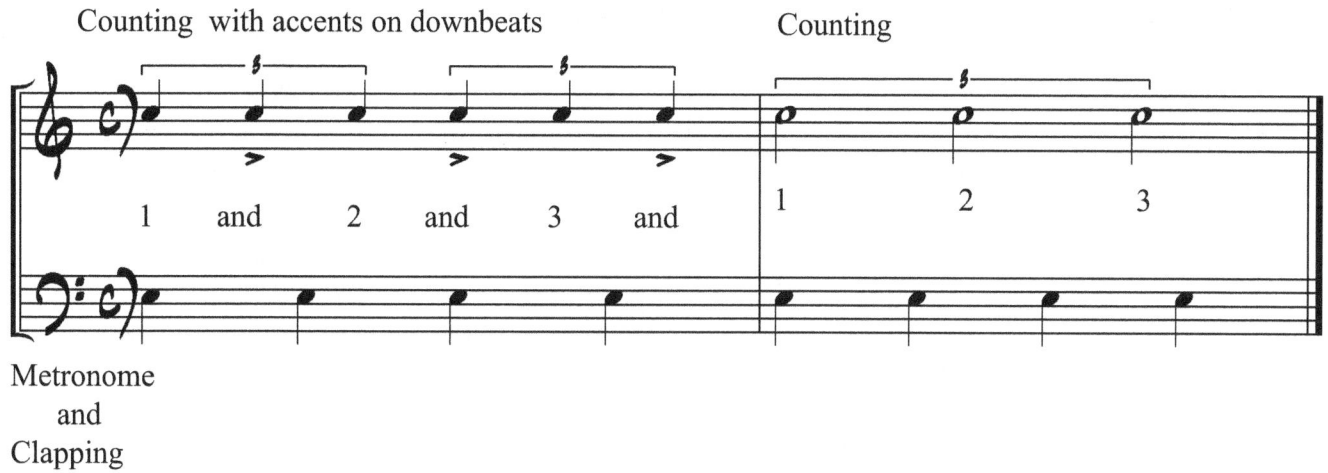

Example 3) and 4) how the superimposed feel of half note triplets is simply translated to our new 3/4 feel; and how dotted quarter notes can be interpreted in our new 3/4 feel.

An important point to remember, and develop, is your complete understanding of how our half note triplet, which has become our new quarter note, can be subdivided as easily, as a quarter note in 4/4. In other words, if one half note triplet equals a quarter note, then we have to understand the subdivision on every level of the quarter note: eighth notes, triplets, sixteens, quintuplets, sextuplets, etc. If our new quarter note is our dotted quarter note, then we have to develop all the subdivisions, of *that* new quarter note. This is how a more fluid, organic phrasing is achieved when working within these new modulations. Each one will require focused study to hear all the different rhythmic levels. Later, dynamics, accents and articulation will help complete the picture.

The following example presents the triplets in our original tempo subdivided into the half note triplet level. The bottom staff presents the harmonic rhythm in our new 3/4 time feel.

Transposed harmonic rhythm.

This next example again presents the eighth note triplets in our original tempo subdivided to represent the rhythmic shape of the melody ("Blues for Alice") as it would be written in our superimposed 3/4 feel. The bottom staff represents the melody notes connected to our subdivisions. Measure #8 is slightly adjusted in the eighth to have note level to reflect it's transposed phrasing in 3/4.

These exercises are to be practiced moving from one level to the next; each level should be repeated a fixed number of times. The metronome should be set to quarter notes. Introducing quintuplets and septuplets will add to both the phrasing and understanding of the basic quarter note simultaneously. Compound rhythmic forms are very prevalent in all forms of music, and it is important to focus on rhythmic accuracy and articulation when studying these subdivisions. Each example presents the subdivisions on the sixteenth note level: 5 or 7 beats for each quarter note; the eighth note level: 5 over 2 (quarter notes) or 7 over 2 (quarter notes); the quarter note level: 5 over 4 (quarter notes) and 7 over 4 (quarter notes); and the half note level: 5 over 8 (quarter notes); and 7 over 8 (quarter notes).

This example presents the sixteenth note quintuplets on the upper ledger line connected (approximately) to the melody notes from the first 4 measures from "Blues for Alice". The melody is written within the 5/4 meter modulation, and the bottom staff shows the harmonic rhythm in the 5/4 meter modulation in the 3-2 subdivision. The subdivision can also be written as a 2-3 subdivision, as well as all the combinations in the previous chapter on compound rhythms.

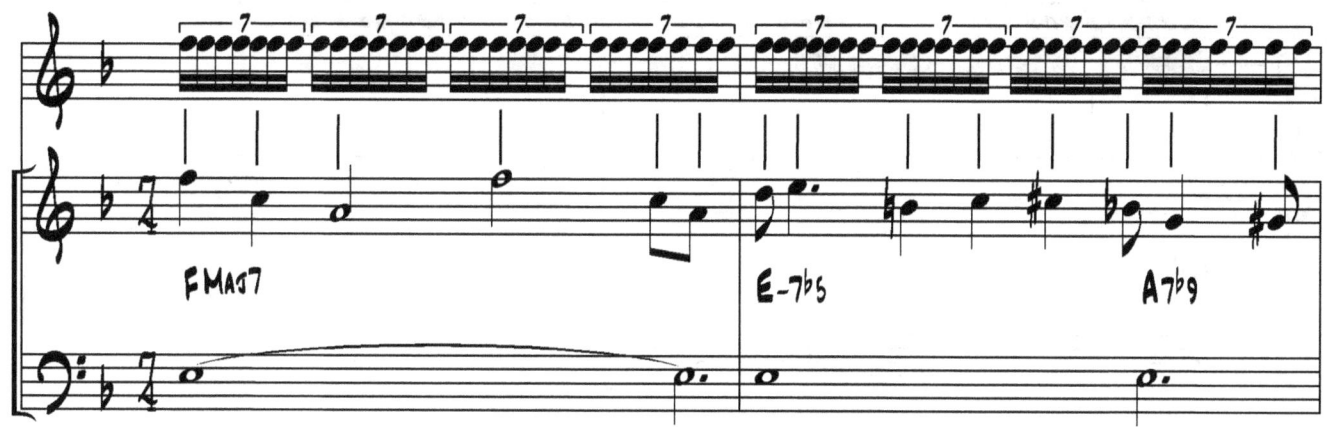

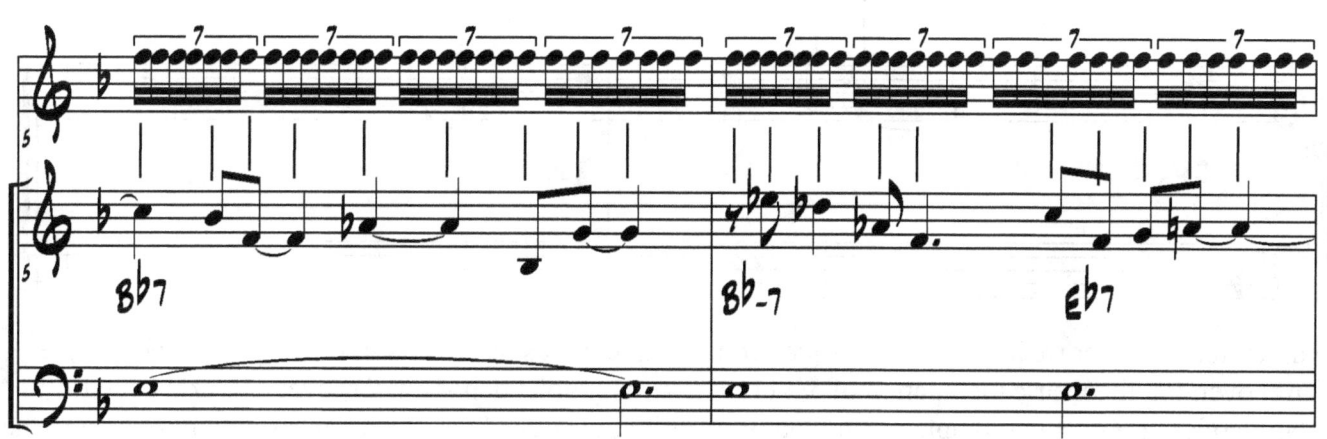

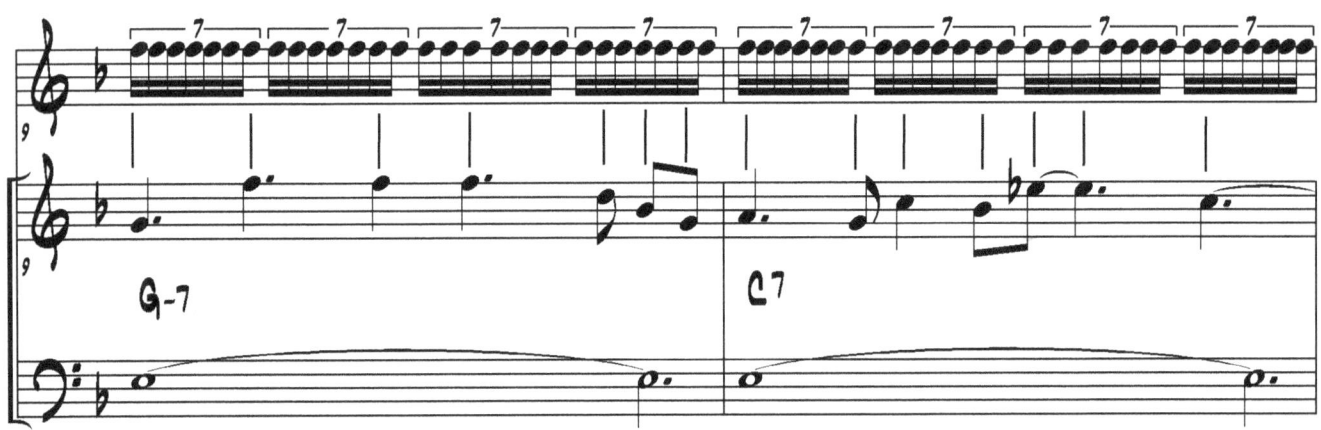

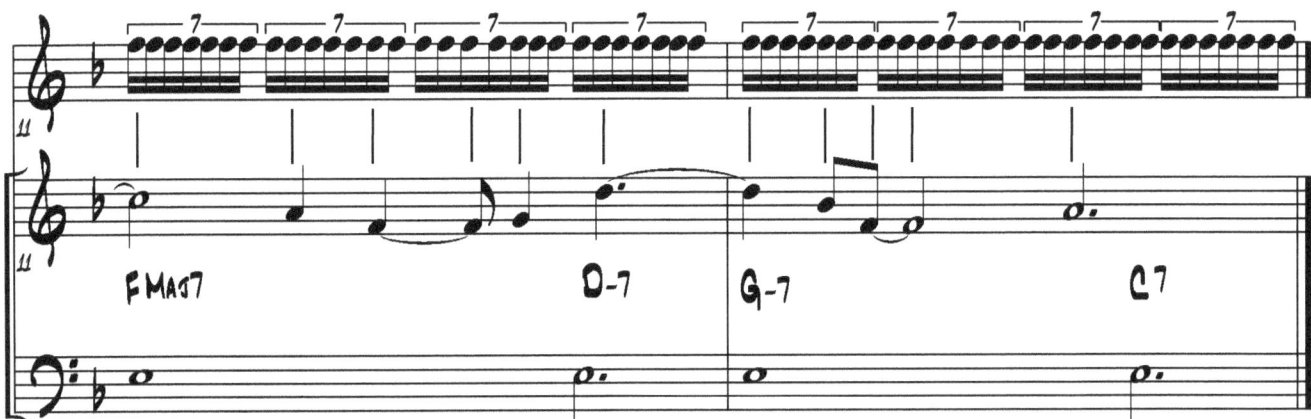

Remember, that whether we impose the six (quarter note triplet phrasing) over 4/4, the three (half note triplet phrasing) over 4/4, the metric modulation of 5/4 (16th note quintuplet denominator) over 4/4, or the metric modulation of 7/4 (16th note septuplet denominator) over 4/4, the downbeat of each measure will remain in the same position. So, if the metronome is set at 60bpm in 4/4 the downbeats will be at the same point for each modulation. The effect, of course, will be an increase or decrease of velocity depending on your modulation.

Books Available From
Muse Eek Publishing Company

The Bruce Arnold series of instruction books for guitar are the result of 30 years of teaching. Mr. Arnold, who teaches at New York University and Princeton University has listened to the questions and problems of his students, and written over fifty books addressing the needs of the beginning to advanced student. Written in a direct, friendly and practical manner, each book is structured in such a way as to enable a student to understand, retain and apply musical information. In short, these books teach.

1st Steps for a Beginning Guitarist
Spiral Bound ISBN 1890944-90-4   Perfect Bound ISBN 1890944-93-9

1st Steps for a Beginning Guitarist is a comprehensive method for guitar students who have no prior musical training. Whether you are playing acoustic, electric or twelve-string guitar, this book will give you the information you need, and trouble shoot the various pitfalls that can hinder the self-taught musician. Includes pictures, videos and audio in the form of midifiles and mp3's.

Chord Workbook for Guitar Volume 1 (2nd edition)
Spiral Bound ISBN 0-9648632-1-9   Perfect Bound ISBN 1890944-50-5

A consistent seller, this book addresses the needs of the beginning through intermediate student. The beginning student will learn chords on the guitar, and a section is also included to help learn the basics of music theory. Progressions are provided to help the student apply these chords to common sequences. The more advanced student will find the reharmonization section to be an invaluable resource of harmonic choices. Information is given through musical notation as well as tablature.

Chord Workbook for Guitar Volume 2 (2nd edition)
Spiral Bound ISBN 0-9648632-3-5   Perfect Bound ISBN 1890944-51-3

This book is the Rosetta Stone of pop/jazz chords, and is geared to the intermediate to advanced student. These are the chords that any serious student bent on a musical career must know. Unlike other books which simply give examples of isolated chords, this unique book provides a comprehensive series of progressions and chord combinations which are immediately applicable to both composition and performance.

Music Theory Workbook for Guitar Series

The worlds most popular instrument, the guitar, is not taught in our public schools. In addition, it is one of the hardest on which to learn the basics of music. As a result, it is frequently difficult for the serious guitarist to get a firm foundation in theory.

Theory Workbook for Guitar Volume 1
Spiral Bound ISBN 0-9648632-4-3   Perfect Bound ISBN 1890944-52-1

This book provides real hands-on application of intervals and chords. A theory section written in concise and easy to understand language prepares the student for all exercises. Worksheets are given that quiz a student about intervals and chord construction using staff notation and guitar tablature. Answers are supplied in the back of the book enabling a student to work without a teacher.

Theory Workbook for Guitar Volume 2
Spiral Bound ISBN 0-9648632-5-1   Perfect Bound ISBN 1890944-53-X

This book provides real hands-on application for 22 different scale types. A theory section written in concise and easy to understand language prepares the student for all exercises. Worksheets are given that quiz a student about scale construction using staff notation and guitar tablature. Answers are supplied in the back of the book enabling a student to work without a teacher. Audio files are also available on the muse-eek.com website to facilitate practice and improvisation with all the scales presented.

Rhythm Book Series

These books are a breakthrough in music instruction, using the internet as a teaching tool! Audio files of all the exercises are easily downloaded from the internet.

Rhythm Primer
Spiral Bound ISBN 0-890944-03-3   Perfect Bound ISBN 1890944-59-9

This 61 page book concentrates on all basic rhythms using four rhythmic levels. All examples use one pitch, allowing the student to focus completely on time and rhythm. All exercises can be downloaded from the internet to facilitate learning. See http://www.muse-eek.com for details

Rhythms Volume 1
Spiral Bound ISBN 0-9648632-7-8   Perfect Bound ISBN 1890944-55-6

This 120 page book concentrates on eighth note rhythms and is a thesaurus of rhythmic patterns. All examples use one pitch, allowing the student to focus completely on time and rhythm. All exercises can be downloaded from the internet to facilitate learning. See http://www.muse-eek.com for details.

Rhythms Volume 2
Spiral Bound ISBN 0-9648632-8-6   Perfect Bound ISBN 1890944-56-4

This volume concentrates on sixteenth note rhythms, and is a 108 page thesaurus of rhythmic patterns. All examples use one pitch, allowing the student to focus completely on time and rhythm. All exercises can be downloaded from the internet to facilitate learning. See http://www.muse-eek.com for details.

Rhythms Volume 3
Spiral Bound ISBN 0-890944-04-1   Perfect Bound ISBN 1890944-57-2

This volume concentrates on thirty second note rhythms, and is a 102 page thesaurus of rhythmic patterns. All examples use one pitch, allowing the student to focus completely on time and rhythm. All exercises can be downloaded from the internet to facilitate learning. See http://www.muse-eek.com for details.

Odd Meters Volume 1
Spiral Bound ISBN 0-9648632-9-4   Perfect Bound ISBN 1890944-58-0

This book applies both eighth and sixteenth note rhythms to odd meter combinations. All examples use one pitch, allowing the student to focus completely on time and rhythm. Exercises can be downloaded from the internet to facilitate learning. This 100 page book is an essential sight reading tool. See http://www.muse-eek.com for details.

Contemporary Rhythms Volume 1
Spiral Bound ISBN 1-890944-27-0   Perfect Bound ISBN 1890944-84-X

This volume concentrates on eight note rhythms and is a thesaurus of rhythmic patterns. Each exercise uses one pitch which allows the student to focus completely on time and rhythm. Exercises use modern innovations common to twentieth century notation, thereby familiarizing the student with the most sophisticated systems likely to be encountered in the course of a musical career. All exercises can be downloaded from the internet to facilitate learning. See http://www.muse-eek.com for details.

Contemporary Rhythms Volume 2
Spiral Bound ISBN 1-890944-28-9   Perfect Bound ISBN 1890944-85-8

This volume concentrates on sixteenth note rhythms and is a thesaurus of rhythmic patterns. Each exercise uses one pitch which allows the student to focus completely on time and rhythm. Exercise use modern innovations common to twentieth century notation, thereby familiarizing the student with the most sophisticated systems likely to be encountered in the course of a musical career. All exercises can be downloaded from the internet to facilitate learning. See http://www.muse-eek.com for details.

Independence Volume 1
Spiral Bound ISBN 1-890944-00-9   Perfect Bound ISBN 1890944-83-1

This 51 page book is designed for pianists, stick and touchstyle guitarists, percussionists and anyone who wishes to develop the rhythmic independence of their hands. This volume concentrates on quarter, eighth and sixteenth note rhythms and is a thesaurus of rhythmic patterns. The exercises in this book gradually incorporate more and more complex rhythmic patterns making it an excellent tool for both the beginning and the advanced student.

Other Guitar Study Aids

Right Hand Technique for Guitar Volume 1
Spiral Bound ISBN 0-9648632-6-X   Perfect Bound ISBN 1890944-54-8

Heres a breakthrough in music instruction, using the internet as a teaching tool! This book gives a concise method for developing right hand technique on the guitar, one of the most overlooked and under-addressed aspects of learning the instrument. The simplest, most basic movements are used to build fatigue-free technique. Exercises can be downloaded from the internet to facilitate learning. See http://www.muse-eek.com for details.

Single String Studies Volume One
Spiral Bound ISBN 1-890944-01-7   Perfect Bound ISBN 1890944-62-9

This book is an excellent learning tool for both the beginner who has no experience reading music on the guitar, and the advanced student looking to improve their ledger line reading and general knowledge of each string of the guitar. Each exercise concentrates the students attention on one string at a time. This allows a familiarity to form between the written pitch and where it can be found on the guitar along with improving ones feel for jumping linearly across the fretboard. Exercises can be downloaded from the internet to facilitate learning. See http://www.muse-eek.com for details.

Single String Studies Volume Two
Spiral Bound ISBN 1-890944-05-X   Perfect Bound ISBN 1890944-64-5

      This book is a continuation of Volume One, but using non-diatonic notes. Volume Two helps the intermediate and advanced student improve their ledger line reading and general knowledge of each string of the guitar. Each exercise concentrates the students attention on one string at a time. This allows a familiarity to form between the written pitch and where it can be found on the guitar along with improving ones feel for jumping linearly across the fretboard. Exercises can be downloaded from the internet to facilitate learning. See http://www.muse-eek.com for details.

Single String Studies Volume One (Bass Clef)
Spiral Bound ISBN 1-890944-02-5   Perfect Bound ISBN 1890944-63-7

      This book is an excellent learning tool for both the beginner who has no experience reading music on the bass guitar, and the advanced student looking to improve their ledger line reading and general knowledge of each string of the bass. Each exercise concentrates a students attention of one string at a time. This allows a familiarity to form between the written pitch and where it can be found on the bass along with improving ones feel for jumping linearly across the fretboard. Exercises can be downloaded from the internet to facilitate learning. See http://www.muse-eek.com for details.

Single String Studies Volume Two (Bass Clef)
Spiral Bound ISBN 1-890944-06-8   Perfect Bound ISBN 1890944-65-3

      This book is a continuation of Volume One, but using non-diatonic notes. Volume Two helps the intermediate and advanced student improve their ledger line reading and general knowledge of each string of the bass. Each exercise concentrates the students attention on one string at a time. This allows a familiarity to form between the written pitch and where it can be found on the bass along with improving ones feel for jumping linearly across the fretboard. Exercises can be downloaded from the internet to facilitate learning. See http://www.muse-eek.com for details.

Guitar Clinic
Spiral Bound ISBN 1-890944-45-9   Perfect Bound ISBN 1890944-86-6

      Guitar Clinic contains techniques and exercises Mr. Arnold uses in the clinics and workshops he teaches around the U.S.. Much of the material in this book is culled from Mr. ArnoldÕs educational series, over thirty books in all. The student wishing to expand on his or her studies will find suggestions within the text as to which of Mr. Arnold's books will best serve their specific needs. Topics covered include: how to read music, sight reading, reading rhythms, music theory, chord and scale construction, modal sequencing, approach notes, reharmonization, bass and chord comping, and hexatonic scales.

The Essentials: Chord Charts, Scales, and Lead Patterns for the Guitar
Saddle Stitched (Stapled) ISBN 1-890944-94-7

      This book is truly essential to the aspiring guitarist. It includes the most commonly played chords on the guitar in all keys, plus a bonus of the most commonly used scales and lead patterns. You can quickly learn all the chords, scales and lead patterns you need to know to play your favorite songs-and solo over them, too! The Essentials doesn't stop there, though. It also includes chord progressions to help you learn how to chord songs in folk, country, rock, blues and other popular styles. The books contain loads of easy to understand diagrams of chords, scales and lead patterns so you will be up and running in no time!

Sight Singing and Ear Training Series

The world is full of ear training and sight reading books, so why do we need more? This sight singing and ear training series uses a different method of teaching relative pitch sight singing and ear training. The success of this method has been remarkable. Along with a new method of ear training these books also use CDs and the internet as a teaching tool! Audio files of all the exercises are easily downloaded from the internet at www.muse-eek.com By combining interactive audio files with a new approach to ear training a studentÕs progress is limited only by their willingness to practice!

A Fanatic's Guide to Ear Training and Sight Singing
Spiral Bound ISBN 1-890944-19-X   Perfect Bound ISBN 1890944-75-0

This book and CD present a method for developing good pitch recognition through sight singing. This method differs from the myriad of other sight singing books in that it develops the ability to identify and name all twelve pitches within a key center. Through this method a student gains the ability to identify sound based on it's relationship to a key and not the relationship of one note to another (i.e. interval training as commonly taught in many texts). All note groupings from one to six notes are presented giving the student a thesaurus of basic note combinations which develops sight singing and note recognition to a level unattainable before this Guide's existence.

Key Note Recognition
Spiral Bound ISBN 1-890944-30-3   Perfect Bound ISBN 1890944-77-7

This book and CD present a method for developing the ability to recognize the function of any note against a key. This method is a must for anyone who wishes to sound one note on an instrument or voice and instantly know what key a song is in. Through this method a student gains the ability to identify a sound based on its relationship to a key and not the relationship of one note to another (i.e. interval training as commonly taught in many texts). Key Center Recognition is a definite requirement before proceeding to two note ear training.

LINES Volume One: Sight Reading and Sight Singing Exercises
Spiral Bound ISBN 1-890944-09-2   Perfect Bound ISBN 1890944-76-9

This book can be used for many applications. It is an excellent source for easy half note melodies that a beginner can use to learn how to read music or for sight singing slightly chromatic lines. An intermediate or advanced student will find exercises for multi-voice reading. These exercises can also be used for multi-voice ear training. The book has the added benefit in that all exercises can be heard by downloading the audio files for each example. See http://www.muse-eek.com for details.

LINES Volume Two: Sight Reading and Sight Singing Exercises
Spiral Bound ISBN 1-594899-88-6   Perfect Bound ISBN 1594899-99-1

Recommended for those who have completed volume one, volume two introduces more complex harmonic material. This book can be used for many applications. It is an excellent source for easy quarter note melodies that a beginner can use to learn how to read music or for sight singing slightly chromatic lines. An intermediate or advanced student will find exercises for multi-voice reading. These exercises can also be used for multi-voice ear training. The book has the added benefit in that all exercises can be heard by downloading the audio files for each example. See http://www.muse-eek.com for details.

Ear Training ONE NOTE: Beginning Level
Spiral Bound ISBN 1-890944-12-2   Perfect Bound ISBN 1890944-66-1

This Book and Audio CD presents a new and exciting method for developing relative pitch ear training. It has been used with great success and is now finally available on CD. There are three levels available depending on the student's ability. This beginning level is recommended for students who have little or no music training.

Ear Training ONE NOTE: Intermediate Level
Spiral Bound ISBN 1-890944-13-0   Perfect Bound ISBN 1890944-67-X

This Audio CD and booklet presents a new and exciting method of developing relative pitch ear training. It has been used with great success and is now finally available on CD. This intermediate level is recommended for students who have had some music training but still find their skills need more development.

Ear Training ONE NOTE: Advanced Level
Spiral Bound ISBN 1-890944-14-9   Perfect Bound ISBN 1890944-68-8

This Audio CD and booklet presents a new and exciting method of developing relative pitch ear training. It has been used with great success and is now finally available on CD. There are three levels available depending on the student's ability. This advanced level is recommended for students who have worked with the intermediate level and now wish to perfect their skills.

Ear Training TWO NOTE: Beginning Level Volume One
Spiral Bound ISBN 1-890944-31-9   Perfect Bound ISBN 1890944-69-6

This Book and Audio CD continues the method of developing relative pitch ear training as set forth in the "Ear Training, One Note" series. There are six volumes in the beginning level series. Through practice, the student eventually gains the ability to recognize the key and the names of any two notes played simultaneously. Volume One concentrates on 5ths. Prerequisite: a strong grasp of the One Note method.

Ear Training TWO NOTE: Beginning Level Volume Two
Spiral Bound ISBN 1-890944-32-7   Perfect Bound ISBN 1890944-70-X

This Book and Audio CD continues the method of developing relative pitch ear training as set forth in the "Ear Training, One Note" series. There are six volumes in the beginning level series. Through practice, the student eventually gains the ability to recognize the key and the names of any two notes played simultaneously. Volume Two concentrates on 3rds. Prerequisite: a strong grasp of the One Note method.

Ear Training TWO NOTE: Beginning Level Volume Three
Spiral Bound ISBN 1-890944-33-5   Perfect Bound ISBN 1890944-71-8

This Book and Audio CD continues the method of developing relative pitch ear training as set forth in the "Ear Training, One Note" series. There are six volumes in the beginning level series. Through practice, the student eventually gains the ability to recognize the key and the names of any two notes played simultaneously. Volume Three concentrates on 6ths. Prerequisite: a strong grasp of the One Note method.

Ear Training TWO NOTE: Beginning Level Volume Four
Spiral Bound ISBN 1-890944-34-3   Perfect Bound ISBN 1890944-72-6

This Book and Audio CD continues the method of developing relative pitch ear training as set forth in the "Ear Training, One Note" series. There are six volumes in the beginning level series. Through practice, the student eventually gains the ability to recognize the key and the names of any two notes played simultaneously. Volume Four concentrates on 4ths. Prerequisite: a strong grasp of the One Note method.

Ear Training TWO NOTE: Beginning Level Volume Five
Spiral Bound ISBN 1-890944-35-1   Perfect Bound ISBN 1890944-73-4

This Book and Audio CD continues the method of developing relative pitch ear training as set forth in the "Ear Training, One Note" series. There are six volumes in the beginning level series. Through practice, the student eventually gains the ability to recognize the key and the names of any two notes played simultaneously. Volume Five concentrates on 2nds. Prerequisite: a strong grasp of the One Note method.

Ear Training TWO NOTE: Beginning Level Volume Six
Spiral Bound ISBN 1-890944-36-X   Perfect Bound ISBN 1890944-74-2

This Book and Audio CD continues the method of developing relative pitch ear training as set forth in the "Ear Training, One Note" series. There are six volumes in the beginning level series. Through practice, the student eventually gains the ability to recognize the key and the names of any two notes played simultaneously. Volume Six concentrates on 7ths. Prerequisite: a strong grasp of the One Note method.

Comping Styles Series

This series is built on the progressions found in Chord Workbook Volume One. Each book covers a specific style of music and presents exercises to help a guitarist, bassist or drummer master that style. Audio CDs are also available so a student can play along with each example and really get "into the groove."

Comping Styles for the Guitar Volume Two FUNK
Spiral Bound ISBN 1-890944-07-6   Perfect Bound ISBN 1890944-60-2

This volume teaches a student how to play guitar or piano in a funk style. 36 Progressions are presented: 12 keys of a Major and Minor Blues plus 12 keys of Rhythm Changes A different groove is presented for each exercise giving the student a wide range of funk rhythms to master. An Audio CD is also included so a student can play along with each example and really get "into the groove." The audio CD contains "trio" versions of each exercise with Guitar, Bass and Drums.

Comping Styles for the Bass Volume Two FUNK
Spiral Bound ISBN 1-890944-08-4   Perfect Bound ISBN 1890944-61-0

This volume teaches a student how to play bass in a funk style. 36 Progressions are presented: 12 keys of a Major and Minor Blues plus 12 keys of Rhythm Changes A different groove is presented for each exercise giving the student a wide range of funk rhythms to master. An Audio CD is also included so a student can play along with each example and really get "into the groove." The audio CD contains "trio" versions of each exercise with Guitar, Bass and Drums.

Jazz and Blues Bass Line
Spiral Bound ISBN 1-890944-15-7   Perfect Bound ISBN 1890944-16-5

This book covers the basics of bass line construction. A theoretical guide to building bass lines is presented along with 36 chord progressions utilizing the twelve keys of a Major and Minor Blues, plus twelve keys of Rhythm Changes. A reharmonization section is also provided which demonstrates how to reharmonize a chord progression on the spot.

Time Series

The Doing Time series presents a method for contacting, developing and relying on your internal time sense: This series is an excellent resource for any musician who is serious about developing strong internal sense of time. This is particularly useful in any kind of music where the rhythms and time signatures may be very complex or free, and there is no conductor.

THE BIG METRONOME
Spiral Bound ISBN 1-890944-37-8   Perfect Bound ISBN 1890944-82-3

The Big Metronome is designed to help you develop a better internal sense of time. This is accomplished by requiring you to "feel time" rather than having you rely on the steady click of a metronome. The idea is to slowly wean yourself away from an external device and rely on your internal/natural sense of time. The exercises presented work in conjunction with the three CDs that accompany this book. CD 1 presents the first 13 settings from a traditional metronome 40-66; the second CD contains metronome markings 69-116, and the third CD contains metronome markings 120-208. The first CD gives you a 2 bar count off and a click every measure, the second CD gives you a 2 bar count off and a click every 2 measures, the 3rd CD gives you a 2 bar count off and a click every 4 measures. By presenting all common metronome markings a student can use these 3 CDs as a replacement for a traditional metronome.

Doing Time with the Blues Volume One
Spiral Bound ISBN 1-890944-17-3   Perfect Bound ISBN 1890944-78-5

The book and CD presents a method for gaining an internal sense of time thereby eliminating dependence on a metronome. The book presents the basic concept for developing good time and also includes exercises that can be practiced with the CD. The CD provides eight 8 minute tracks at different tempos in which the time is delineated every 2 bars, and with an extra hit every 12 bars to outline the blues form. The student may then use the exercises presented in the book to gain control of their execution or improvise to gain control of their ideas using this bare minimum of time delineation.

Doing Time with the Blues Volume Two
Spiral Bound ISBN 1-890944-18-1   Perfect Bound ISBN 1890944-79-3

This is the 2nd volume of a four volume series which presents a method for developing a musicians internal sense of time, thereby eliminating dependence on a metronome. This 2nd volume presents different exercises which further the development of this time sense. This 2nd volume begins to test even a professional level players ability. The CD provides eight 8 minute tracks at different tempos in which the time is delineated every 4 bars with an extra hit every 12 bars to outline the blues form. New exercises are also included that can be practiced with the CD. This series is an excellent resource for any musician who is serious about developing an internal sense of time.

Doing Time with 32 Bars Volume One
Spiral Bound ISBN 1-890944-22-X   Spiral Bound ISBN 1890944-80-7

The book and CD presents a method for gaining an internal sense of time thereby eliminating dependence on a metronome. The book presents the basic concept for developing good time and also includes exercises that can be practiced with the CD. The CD provides eight 8 minute tracks at different tempos in which the time is delineated every 2 bars, with an extra hit every 32 to outline the 32 bar form. The student may then use the exercises presented in the book to gain control of their execution or improvise to gain control of their ideas using this bare minimum of time delineation.

Doing Time with 32 Bars Volume Two
Spiral Bound ISBN 1-890944-23-8   Spiral Bound ISBN 1890944-81-5

This is the 2nd volume of a four volume series which presents a method for developing a musicians internal sense of time, thereby eliminating dependence on a metronome.. This 2nd volume presents different exercises which further the development of this time sense. This 2nd volume begins to test even a professional level players ability. The CD provides eight 8 minute tracks at different tempos in which the time is delineated every 4 bars with an extra hit every 32 bars to outline the 32 bar form. New exercises are also included that can be practiced with the CD. This series is an excellent resource for any musician who is serious about developing an internal sense of time.

Time Transformation
Spiral Bound ISBN 1594899-929-0   Perfect Bound ISBN 1594899-930-4

"Time Transformation" is designed to take the application of odd meters to another level of mastery. Etudes are presented in 12 keys using the time signatures of 3/4, 4/4, 5/4, 6/4 and 7/4. There are a total of 60 highly syncopated studies that are presented using various combinations of eighth note and sixteenth note rhythms. Book also includes downloadable "vamps" that can be used in various ways with each étude.

                              Other Workbooks

Music Theory Workbook for All Instruments, Volume 1: Interval and Chord Construction
Spiral Bound ISBN 1594899-51-7   Perfect Bound ISBN 1890944-46-7

This book provides real hands-on application of intervals and chords. A theory section written in concise and easy to understand language prepares the student for all exercises. Worksheets are given that quiz a student about intervals and chord construction using staff notation. Answers are supplied in the back of the book enabling a student to work without a teacher.

Jazz Piano Vocabulary by Roberta Piket, Volume 1: The Major Scale
Spiral Bound ISBN 1594899-51-7   Perfect Bound ISBN 1594899-51-7

This is the 1st volume in a series designed to help the student of jazz piano learn and apply jazz scales by mastering each scale and its uses in improvisation. Each book focuses on a different scale, illustrating the scale in all twelve keys with complete fingerings. Also provided are chords and left hand voicings to match, exercises and études to apply the material to improvising, ideas for further study and listening, and detailed suggestions on how to prace the material. Volume 1 also includes a detailed primer in note reading, basic theory, and rhythmic notation.

Jazz Piano Vocabulary by Roberta Piket, Volume 2: The Dorian Mode
Spiral Bound ISBN 1890944-96-3   Perfect Bound ISBN 1890944-98-X

The 2nd volume in the series, this book focuses on the Dorian scale and applies it to improvising on minor seventh chords. The Dorian scale is presented in all twelve keys with complete fingerings. The book also contains left hand voicings, exercises, many examples, an étude to help apply the material, ideas for further study, an extended discography, and detailed instruction and practice tips.

Jazz Piano Vocabulary by Roberta Piket, Volume 3: The Phrygian Mode
Spiral Bound ISBN 1594899-53-3   Perfect Bound ISBN 1594899-54-1

For students who have covered the basics in Volume 1,2 and 5, this book focuses in the Phrygian and Spanish Phrygian scales. It discuesss "modern" jazz chords such as the "Phrygian" chord (susb9). The scale is presented in all 12 keys with fingerings. It also provides a detailed treatise on a modal approach to chord voicings, practice tips and a Phrygian étude.

Jazz Piano Vocabulary by Roberta Piket, Volume 4: The Lydian Mode
Spiral Bound ISBN 1594899-55-X   Perfect Bound ISBN 1594899-56-8

Volume 4 features the Lydian scale in all twelve keys; two octaves up and down with complete piano fingerings. Chords are presented with left hand voicings that work with the scale (along with fingerings) Also included are exercises to develop the concept of melodic phrasing in improvisation, examples of the use of the Lydian scale in the jazz repertoire, and detailed instructions on how to practice the material. Added feature: author can be contacted online if questions arise.

Jazz Piano Vocabulary by Roberta Piket, Volume 5: The Mixolydian Mode
Spiral Bound ISBN 1594899-57-6   Perfect Bound ISBN 1594899-58-4

This book focuses on the Mixolydian scale and applies it to improvising on dominant seventh and dominant seventh sus chords. The scale is presented in all twelve keys with fingerings. The book also contains an introduction to approach notes, an explanation and étude on twelve bar blues form, left hand voicings, exercises, melodic examples, instruction and practice tips.

Guitar Method Series

This series of books distills several of our previous publications into a method currently in use at New York University for the Summer Guitar Intensive Program. Content is geared towards any musician that is looking to expand their understanding of typical musical concepts but also covers many musically uncharted territories. Material concentrates on essential information the student must master in order to become a professional guitarist in the heavily competitive New York City music scene. This series of books starts with the most basic beginning guitar information and takes the reader to the most advanced musical concepts.

New York Guitar Method Primer Book 1
Spiral Bound ISBN 159489-911-8 Perfect Bound ISBN 159489-912-6

This book provides students with an excellent foundation in theory, ear training, chord and scale comprehension on the guitar. It is a prerequisite for entering New York University's Summer Guitar Intensive Program and provides students studying independently with the tools they will need to successfully move on to Primer Book 2.

New York Guitar Method Primer Book 2
Spiral Bound ISBN 159489-915-0   Perfect Bound ISBN 159489-916-9

This book provides students with an excellent foundation in theory, ear training, chord and scale comprehension on the guitar. It is a prerequisite for entering New York University's Summer Guitar Intensive Program and provides students studying independently with the tools they will need to successfully move on to New York Guitar Method Book 1. "New York Guitar Method Primer Ensemble Book Two" is the companion book for "New York Guitar Method Primer Book Two." This book contains music examples of the information covered in this book so that a student can apply the information through memorization and sight reading.

New York Guitar Method Primer Ensemble Book 2
Spiral Bound ISBN 159489-913-4   Perfect Bound ISBN 159489-914-2

This book is a prerequisite for entering New York University's Summer Guitar Intensive Program and provides students studying independently with the tools they will need to successfully move on to Volume 1. Our Ensemble Method presents a breakthrough approach for teaching guitarist how to sightread. Each chapter has eighth note, sixteenth note, single string, lines, and chord exercises. The book also includes modal jazz vamps and solos and is an excellent resource for lab/ensemble studies as it contains 3 and 4-part reading examples.

New York Guitar Method Volume 1
Spiral Bound ISBN 159489-987-8   Perfect Bound ISBN 159489-900-2

This book contains 22 scales and their theory which are covered in great detail. Multiple types of chord voicings along with an in-Depth coverage of articulations. The application of scales through modal sequences is also explained. The following musical concepts are covered: Finding the Right Scale for Any Chord, Finding the Natural Scale Sound, Thinking the Way You Hear, Two to Eleven Note Scale Possibilities along with a list of 2,048 Scale Possibilities which contain the root. Slash Chords, Regular Chords and Slash Chords, Slash Chord Possibilities, Reharmonization Theory, Adding Tensions.
    "New York Guitar Method Ensemble Book One" is the companion book for "New York Guitar Method Volume One." This book contains music examples of the information covered in this book so that a student can apply the information through memorization and sight reading.

New York Guitar Method Ensemble Book 1
Spiral Bound ISBN 159489-905-3   Perfect Bound ISBN 159489-906-1

Volume One focuses on reading jazz solos that demonstrate the many uses of scales as discussed in the accompanying New York Guitar Method Volume 1. The book also includes jazz and classical reading études and is an excellent resource for lab/ensemble studies as it contains 3 and 4-part reading examples.

New York Guitar Method Volume 2
Spiral Bound ISBN 159489-901-0   Perfect Bound ISBN 159489-902-9

This is the second book in our series currently in use at New York University for the Summer Guitar Intensive Program. A continuation of Volume 1, Volume 2 focuses on approach notes and discusses how to apply approaches to jazz lines in order to create the signature sounding lines of bebop through the contemporary sounding lines of the modern masters. "New York Guitar Method Ensemble Book Two" is the companion book for "New York Guitar Method Volume Two." This book contains music examples of the information covered in this book so that a student can apply the information through memorization and sight reading.

New York Guitar Method Ensemble Book 2
Spiral Bound ISBN 159489-907-X   Perfect Bound ISBN 159489-908-8

Volume Two focuses on reading jazz solos that demonstrate the many uses of approach notes as discussed in the accompanying New York Guitar Method Volume 2. The book also includes jazz and classical reading études and is an excellent resource for lab/ensemble studies as it contains 3 and 4-part reading examples.

Set Theory Method

This series of books explores the relationships of post tonal theory to contemporary improvisation. It is meant to bridge the gap between jazz theory and contemporary set theory.

Sonic Resource Guide
Spiral Bound ISBN 159489-933-9   Perfect Bound ISBN 159489-934-7

"Set Theory for Improvisation" examines the use and organization of pitch class sets for improvisation and composition. Two through twelve note pitch class sets are explored and their application to the harmony and melody shown through multiple examples. The companion series "Set Theory for Improvisation Ensemble" is recommended as both a overall musical development tool and as a sight reading gold mine. For all instruments.

Set Theory for Improvisation Ensemble Method

The ensemble method gives examples of applying post tonal theory to contemporary improvisation in the form of études. Each étude explores the melodic possibilities using various combinations of note groupings, rhythms, metric level, melodic range and density. There are 12 études in each book, one in each key which can be played over a variety of chords. These études range from highly diatonic to non-diatonic examples depending on the organization of the material. For all instruments.

Set Theory for Improvisation Ensemble Method: Hexatonic 027 027
Spiral Bound ISBN 159489-920-7   Perfect Bound ISBN 159489-921-5

Set Theory for Improvisation Ensemble Method: Hexatonic 027 016
Spiral Bound ISBN 159489-922-3   Perfect Bound ISBN 159489-923-1

Set Theory for Improvisation Ensemble Method: Hexatonic 027 026
Spiral Bound ISBN 159489-924-X   Perfect Bound ISBN 159489-925-8

E-Books

The Bruce Arnold series of instructional E-books is for the student who wishes to target specific areas of study that are of particular interest. Many of these books are excerpted from other larger texts. The excerpted source is listed for each book. These books are available on-line at www.muse-eek.com as well as at many e-tailers throughout the internet. These books can also be purchased in the traditional book binding format. (See the ISBN number for proper format)

Chord Velocity: Volume One, Learning to switch between chords quickly
E-book ISBN 1-890944-88-2   Traditional Book Binding ISBN 1-890944-97-1

The first hurdle a beginning guitarist encounters is difficulty in switching between chords quickly enough to make a chord progression sound like music. This book provides exercises that help a student gradually increase the speed with which they change chords. Special free audio files are also available on the muse-eek.com website to make practice more productive and fun. Within a few weeks, remarkable improvement can be achieved using this method. This book is excerpted from "1st Steps for a Beginning Guitarist Volume One."

Guitar Technique: Volume One, Learning the basics to fast, clean, accurate and fluid performance skills.
E-book ISBN 1-890944-91-2   Traditional Book Binding ISBN 1-890944-99-8

This book is for both the beginning guitarist or the more experienced guitarist who wishes to improve their technique. All aspects of the physical act of playing the guitar are covered, from how to hold a guitar to the specific way each hand is involved in the playing process. Pictures and videos are provided to help clarify each technique. These pictures and videos are either contained in the book or can be downloaded at www.muse-eek.com This book is excerpted from "1st Steps for a Beginning Guitarist Volume One."

Accompaniment: Volume One, Learning to Play Bass and Chords Simultaneously
E-book ISBN 1-890944-87-4   Traditional Book Binding ISBN 1-890944-96-3

The techniques found within this book are an excellent resource for creating and understanding how to play bass and chords simultaneously in a jazz or blues style. Special attention is paid to understanding how this technique is created, thereby enabling the student to recreate this style with other pieces of music. This book is excerpted from the book "Guitar Clinic."

Beginning Rhythm Studies: Volume One, Learning the basics of reading rhythm and playing in time.
E-book ISBN 1-890944-89-0   Traditional Book Binding 1-890944-98-X

This book covers the basics for anyone wishing to understand or improve their rhythmic abilities. Simple language is used to show the student how to read and play rhythm. Exercises are presented which can accelerate the learning process. Audio examples in the form of midifiles are available on the muse-eek.com website to facilitate learning the correct rhythm in time. This book is excerpted from the book "Rhythm Primer."

www.ingramcontent.com/pod-product-compliance
Lightning Source LLC
Chambersburg PA
CBHW080350170426
43194CB00014B/2744